BASEBALL

BY BO SMOLKA

CONTENT CONSULTANT
MIKE STADLER PhD
ASSOCIATE PROFESSOR OF PSYCHOLOGY
UNIVERSITY OF MISSOURI

Published by ABDO Publishing Company, PO Box 398166, Minneapolis, MN 55439. Copyright © 2012 by Abdo Consulting Group, Inc. International copyrights reserved in all countries. No part of this book may be reproduced in any form without written permission from the publisher. SportsZone™ is a trademark and logo of ABDO Publishing Company.

Printed in the United States of America,
North Mankato, Minnesota
102011
012012

 THIS BOOK CONTAINS AT LEAST 10% RECYCLED MATERIALS.

Editor: Chrös McDougall
Copy Editor: Anna Comstock
Design and Production: Craig Hinton

Photo Credits: Matt Slocum/AP Images, cover (bottom); iStockphoto, cover (top); AP Images, 1, 15, 21, 23, 25, 26, 33, 41, 51, 53, 58 (bottom); Nick Wass/AP Images, 5; John Swart/AP Images, 7; Roberto Borea/AP Images, 8; Tom Olmscheid/AP Images, 11; Brady National Photographic Art Gallery (Washington, D.C.)/Library of Congress, 13, 58 (top); Library of Congress, 18, 58 (middle); Ted Sande/AP Images, 28; National Baseball Hall of Fame, Cooperstown/AP Images, 31; John Rooney/AP Images, 35, 59 (top); Harry Harris/AP Images, 39, 59 (middle); Eric Risberg/AP Images, 42; Craig Fujii/AP Images, 44; Beth A. Keiser/AP Images, 46; Genevieve Ross/AP Images, 48; Charles Rex Arbogast/AP Images, 54; Carlos Osorio/AP Images, 57, 59 (bottom)

Library of Congress Cataloging-in-Publication Data
Smolka, Bo, 1965-.
  Baseball / By Bo Smolka.
     p. cm. -- (Best sport ever)
  Includes index.
  ISBN 978-1-61783-140-9
  1. Baseball--Juvenile literature. I. Title.
  GV867.5.S635 2012
  796.357--dc23
                            2011033254

TABLE of CONTENTS

CHAPTER 1

THE IRON MAN

It was a game like so many others. That is exactly what made it so special. On September 6, 1995, Cal Ripken Jr. trotted out to his position at shortstop for the Baltimore Orioles just as he had done every other game that season. And the season before that. And many more before that.

Ripken had joined the Orioles' starting lineup on May 30, 1982. During the 1983 season, when the Orioles won the World Series, Ripken started every game at shortstop. In 1988, when the Orioles lost 107 of their 161 games, Ripken also started every game. Managers came and went. Teammates came and went. The Orioles even changed stadiums. Yet Ripken kept on playing. As surely as the umpire would shout "Play ball!" to start a game, Ripken would be on the field for the Orioles.

Cal Ripken leaps over Damion Easley of the California Angels and makes the throw to first base in 1995. It was his 2,130th consecutive game played.

Lou Gehrig, the Hall of Fame first baseman for the New York Yankees, played in 2,130 straight Major League Baseball (MLB) games from 1925 to 1939. He was forced to retire by a medical condition now known as Lou Gehrig's disease. Baseball fans thought his streak could never be equaled.

Then along came Ripken. Fans around the country marveled at the durability of the player who came to be known as "The Iron Man." Nothing could stop him. Ripken played through bumps and bruises. He played through slumps and losses. For 15 straight seasons, Ripken played in every game.

And he played very well. Ripken hit at least 20 home runs every year from 1982 to 1991. He drove in more than 100 runs in four different seasons. And he won two Gold Glove Awards, which are given to the top fielder at each position in each league after every season.

A FAMILY AFFAIR

Ripken family life had always revolved around baseball and the Orioles. Cal Ripken Sr. played minor league baseball and then spent 36 years in the Orioles organization. He was a scout, a coach, and then the Orioles' manager in 1987 and briefly in 1988. Cal Sr.'s other son, Billy, was a major league infielder from 1987 to 1998, including seven seasons alongside his brother with the Orioles. In 1987, Cal Ripken Sr. was the Orioles' manager, Cal Ripken Jr. started at shortstop, and Billy Ripken started at second base. That marked the first time in major league history a team had a father managing two sons at the same time.

In just his second season, Cal Ripken led his team to victory over the Philadelphia Phillies in the 1983 World Series.

On August 1, 1994, against the Minnesota Twins, Ripken played in his 2,000th straight game. That summer, though, major league players and owners were locked in a bitter dispute. The owners wanted a salary cap. The players refused.

On August 12, 1994, major league players went on strike. They would not go to work, or in this case, to the ballpark. There would be no more MLB that season. The World Series was canceled.

Players and owners were mad at one another. Fans were mad, too. To them, the strike was pure greed—rich owners fighting with rich players over more money. The average fan who worked

Since Cal Ripken's streak ended, no player has come close to reaching it.

hard to be able to buy tickets to a game had a hard time feeling sympathy for either side.

When the players and owners finally settled the strike in April of 1995, many fans refused to go to games. The strike had left them angry. But Ripken managed to help baseball's damaged image.

As the 1995 season went on, Ripken closed in on Gehrig's streak. The chase captivated baseball fans. So did Ripken's demeanor. Ripken played the game hard. He stayed out of trouble. Home or away, Ripken frequently stayed on the field after games and signed autographs.

Ripken often said the streak was never his motivation. He simply came to work each day ready to do his job. That was something to which the average fan could relate.

Then, on September 6, 1995, in Baltimore, the Orioles hosted the California Angels. As he had done for the previous 2,130 games, Ripken jogged out to his position on the left side of the infield. But this game was special. The sellout crowd that night included President Bill Clinton. He and everyone else were there to see Ripken break Gehrig's record by playing his record 2,131st straight game.

A magical night got even more special in the fourth inning. Ripken drilled a pitch into the left-field seats for a home run. Then, after the Angels batted in the fifth inning, the game was official. If a game is called because of rain before the end of the fifth inning it has to be replayed. Ripken's streak was now the longest in baseball history. Fans gave him a standing ovation.

EXTRA INNINGS

There is no clock in baseball, and there are no ties. A game is played until there is a winner, no matter how long or how many innings that takes. In 1981, the Pawtucket Red Sox and the Rochester Red Wings, two minor league teams, played the longest professional game in history. Pawtucket won, 3–2, in 33 innings. The Rochester third baseman in that game was Cal Ripken.

On his way off the field after the inning, Ripken waved to the crowd and then sat down in the dugout. But fans wanted more. Teammates playfully pushed Ripken out of the dugout. As the crowd roared, Ripken began a slow jog around the warning track, waving and shaking hands with fans in the front row. It was a victory lap for endurance, for desire, and for baseball. The Orioles went on to win the game 4–2.

In a speech on the field after the game, Ripken said, "You are challenged by the game of baseball to do your very best day in and day out. And that's all I've ever tried to do."

Ripken went on to play every game for two more seasons. Then, on September 20, 1998, shortly before the Orioles were to play the New York Yankees, Ripken went to his manager, Ray Miller, and told him it was time. Ripken wanted the night off. The streak was over, after 2,632 straight games. Although the Orioles and Yankees were division rivals, the Yankees' players

TEE TIME

For many kids, their first experience with baseball is playing tee ball. In that game, the ball isn't pitched. It sits on a tee, a player swings at it, and then he runs the bases after hitting the ball. Baseball players never outgrow tee ball. Major league players still use a tee to practice hitting almost every day.

Cal Ripken records hit number 3,000, a single to center field, against the Minnesota Twins on Saturday, April 15, 2000.

stood up and applauded Ripken's streak when they realized he was not in the lineup. So did the fans at Camden Yards in Baltimore.

Ripken played three more seasons, but injuries and age were catching up to the Iron Man. He retired after the 2001 season.

Ripken will always be remembered for his talent. He was a 19-time All-Star and twice the American League (AL) Most Valuable Player (MVP). Ripken will also be remembered for giving angry fans a reason to like baseball again in 1995. But perhaps most of all, he will be remembered for simply showing up at the ballpark, every day, ready to play.

CHAPTER 2

THE EARLY YEARS

The idea of hitting a ball with a bat has been around about as long as there has been a ball and something with which to hit it. Romans and Greeks played stick-and-ball games as far back as 2000 BCE as part of religious ceremonies. And Rounders, another game involving hitting a ball with a bat, has been played in England for at least 300 years.

Abner Doubleday is widely credited with inventing baseball in 1839 in a cow pasture in Cooperstown, New York. That claim, though, might be way off base. There is a reference to US soldiers playing a game of "base" at Valley Forge during the Revolutionary War in 1778. Additionally, many of the rules of baseball that are credited to Doubleday were already being used in a game called town ball.

Credited with inventing America's pastime, Abner Doubleday also served as a Brigadier General in the Federal Army during the American Civil War.

In the 1930s, the first known baseball in the form that we know today was found near Cooperstown. That seemed to support Doubleday's role in the game's birth. But the truth might never be known.

What is known is that in 1845, a group called the New York Knickerbockers formed a baseball club and produced the first written rules. On June 19, 1846, the Knickerbockers played another New York club in Hoboken, New Jersey. It was the first officially recorded baseball game.

The early game did not look much like the game today. Back then, pitchers had to throw underhanded. In addition, any ball caught on the fly or on one bounce was an out. And the first team to score 21 "aces," or runs, was the winner. Many of the original basic rules, though, still exist. Three outs end an inning.

GLOVES

The first baseball players did not use gloves. The first gloves appeared in 1875, approximately 30 years after the first game. Early gloves looked like padded gardening gloves, and players wore them on both hands. Today, many players, particularly from poor areas, learn to play without a glove. Miguel Tejada, an All-Star from the Dominican Republic, did not have a glove until he was 19 years old. Hall of Fame shortstop Ozzie Smith, who became known as one of the greatest fielders of all time, said his first glove was a paper bag.

The original baseball used by Abner Doubleday in 1839 includes many of the same elements found in the modern ball.

A team must stick with a batting order. And a runner can be forced out or tagged out. These current rules were all spelled out in the "Knickerbocker Rules."

By the 1860s, the sport was spreading rapidly. In 1869, the Cincinnati Red Stockings became the first professional team. The Red Stockings recruited the top players and won 57 straight games against teams from around the country. Soon, cities from New York to Illinois were fielding teams. And professional leagues were formed around the United States. There are two major leagues in operation today: the National League (NL), which began in 1876, and the American League (AL), which began in 1901. Other major leagues also existed in the early days. The most prominent was the American Association (1882–91).

THE WORLD SERIES

In baseball's early days, professional leagues came and went. The two that lasted were the AL and the NL. In 1903, the two leagues agreed to have their champions play each other at the end of the season. The World Series was born. The first World Series was a best-of-nine format. The Boston Americans, later known as the Red Sox, beat the Pittsburgh Pirates, five games to three. In 1904, the New York Giants, led by manager John McGraw, won the NL pennant. Boston again won the AL pennant. McGraw, though, did not get along with AL president Ban Johnson, and the Giants refused to play. There was no World Series that year. Since 1905, the World Series has been held every year except the strike-shortened 1994 season.

Changing Rules

The rules and equipment involved in baseball evolved over many years. One of the biggest rule changes came in 1893. The distance from the pitcher's mound to home plate was set at 60 feet, 6 inches (18.44 m). That is still the distance today. Before that, pitchers were just 50 feet (15.24 m) away from the batter.

BALLPARKS

In the infield, every professional ballpark is the same: The bases are always 90 feet (27.43 m) apart and the pitcher's rubber is always 60 feet, 6 inches (18.44 m) from home plate. Other than those requirements, though, every ballpark differs. The distance to the fences differs and the height of the fences differs. Fenway Park, the home of the Boston Red Sox, has one of the most unusual features of any ballpark. The left-field wall is known as "The Green Monster." It is 37 feet (11.28 m) high. Most outfield walls are not even a third of that height.

The time from 1900 to 1919 is known as baseball's "dead ball era." Not many home runs were hit. In 1905, Fred Odwell of the Cincinnati Reds led the major leagues in homers with nine. At that time, ballpark fences—if they existed at all—were much farther from home plate than those found in stadiums today. So teams relied on singles, hit-and-run plays, and stolen bases to score runs.

Pitchers had a couple of other advantages back then that they do not have today. For example, they were allowed to throw spitballs. By adding spit, lotion, tobacco juice, or other lubricants to the surface of the ball, a good pitcher could get the ball to move in crazy ways. Also, a game was often played with just one ball. Batters had to try to hit a dirty, scuffed ball that grew softer as the game wore on. That meant the ball often had a lot of

Pitcher Cy Young is the all-time leader in both victories and complete games pitched. He played for five different teams from 1890 to 1911.

movement, sometimes in fading daylight. No wonder only three AL batters hit better than .300 in 1905. A .300 batting average means a batter gets a hit three times per 10 at-bats.

Scandal at the World Series

The Chicago White Sox emerged as a leading team of the dead ball era. They won the World Series in 1917 and again won the AL pennant in 1919. That team is also linked to baseball's biggest scandal.

The White Sox and the Reds met in the 1919 World Series. The White Sox were expected to win. Right away, however, something was strange. In the first inning of Game 1, White Sox ace pitcher Eddie Cicotte hit Cincinnati's leadoff batter. Cicotte gave up six runs before being taken out in the fourth inning. The White Sox lost, 9–1.

Cincinnati went on to win the best-of-nine series in eight games. That meant they were the first to win five games. Many observers thought the White Sox did not try their hardest. They did not look anything like the team that had an 88–52 record during the regular season.

Apparently they had a reason. Before the series began, eight White Sox players had made a deal with professional gamblers. They would "fix" the World Series. That is, they would be paid by the gamblers to lose on purpose.

CY YOUNG

In baseball's early days, pitchers almost always finished what they started, as relief pitchers were not common yet. Pitching for the Cleveland Spiders in 1892, Cy Young made 49 starts and had 48 complete games. (Starting pitchers take games off to rest between starts; today, starting pitchers start every fourth or fifth game, which is around 30 games per season.) Young's career totals of 511 wins and 749 complete games are records by a large margin. By contrast, in 2010, Roy Halladay led the major leagues in complete games with nine. Today, the Cy Young Award is given out after each season to the best pitcher from both the AL and the NL.

"TAKE ME OUT TO THE BALL GAME"

Jack Norworth wrote the words to the famous baseball song, "Take Me out to the Ball Game," in 1908. Albert von Tilzer wrote the music. Norworth got the idea for the song when he was riding a train in New York and saw posters announcing an upcoming game. When he wrote the song, Norworth had never seen a baseball game.

Cicotte's pitch that hit the first batter in Game 1 was a signal to gamblers: The fix was on.

Over the next year, the truth came out. Baseball commissioner Kenesaw Mountain Landis banned the eight "Black Sox" from baseball for life. The baseball commissioner is the chief executive of MLB.

The most famous of the Black Sox was outfielder "Shoeless Joe" Jackson. For his career, Jackson had a .356 batting average. Through the 2010 season, that remained the third highest in baseball history. Jackson is not in the Hall of Fame, though, because of his role in what is known as the Black Sox Scandal.

Baseball was at a low point. Because of World War I in 1917 and 1918, the US economy was struggling. Many people simply did not have extra money to buy baseball tickets. As such, attendance was down. Interest was down as well. Teams

Joseph "Shoeless Joe" Jackson played an entire game without shoes in 1907 because he had not had the chance to break them in yet.

were losing money. Now, in addition to all of that, players had admitted to fixing games.

Baseball badly needed a boost. And it got a big one in 1920 from a strapping slugger named Babe Ruth.

CHAPTER 3

BASEBALL GOES TO WAR

Baseball's dead ball era ended with a bang in 1920. Before the season began, MLB made two important rules changes. Pitchers could no longer throw spitballs or scuffed balls. And new, cleaner baseballs would be put into play more often.

Hitters loved it. Fans loved it too. Balls started flying out of ballparks in record numbers, especially off the bat of Babe Ruth.

Ruth had begun his major league career as a pitcher with the Boston Red Sox. He later became an outfielder. Playing for the Red Sox in 1919, Ruth smashed a record 29 home runs. That was just a hint of what was to come.

Boston's owner at that time, Harry Frazee, was not a Babe Ruth fan. He thought his star player was a selfish troublemaker.

Before he became the "Sultan of Swat," Babe Ruth won 89 games as a pitcher for the Boston Red Sox. His .671 winning percentage ranks 12th all time.

Plus, Frazee ran a theater business that needed money. So before the 1920 season, Frazee sold Ruth's contract to the New York Yankees for $125,000. The Red Sox's decision is considered one of the worst in sports history.

The "Sultan of Swat"

In 1920, during his first season in New York, Ruth smacked 54 home runs. The next year, he hit 59. Baseball had never before seen anything like him. Fans flocked to ballparks to see the "Sultan of Swat," as he was known. In the first game ever at the original Yankee Stadium, which opened in 1923, Ruth smashed a three-run home run and the Yankees won. Many people called that famous stadium "The House that Ruth Built" because the excitement surrounding Ruth helped lead to its construction.

Led by Ruth, the Yankees became the dominant team of the 1920s. From 1921 to 1928, the Yankees won six AL pennants and

CURSE OF THE BAMBINO

Many years after the Boston Red Sox sold Babe Ruth to the New York Yankees, Red Sox fans began referring to the move as the "Curse of the Bambino." With Ruth, Boston won three World Series titles from 1914 to 1919. After they sold Ruth, Boston went more than 80 years without winning the World Series. Meanwhile, the Yankees won 26 titles during that time.

Tony Lazzeri, *left*, Babe Ruth, *center*, and Lou Gehrig, *right*, hit a combined 125 home runs during the 1927 season as members of "Murderers Row."

three World Series. Their 1927 team might have been the best ever. That team went 110–44 and won the World Series. Few opposing pitchers escaped a pummeling from a lineup that came to be known as "Murderers Row."

The 1927 Yankees had the top three home-run hitters in the AL, led by Ruth's record 60 homers. First baseman Lou Gehrig was second with 47. He also hit .373 with 175 runs batted in (RBIs), a record at that time. Second baseman Tony Lazzeri was

Lou Gehrig, *left*, and Joe DiMaggio, *right*, led the New York Yankees to three consecutive World Series wins from 1936 to 1938.

third in the AL with 18 home runs. Meanwhile, center fielder Earle Combs led the league in hits with 231.

Ruth retired in 1935 as baseball's all-time home-run king with 714 during his career. But if fans thought the Yankees would fade without Ruth, they thought wrong. Led by Gehrig and rookie outfielder Joe DiMaggio, the Yankees won the first of four straight World Series championships in 1936.

The Summer of '41

The Yankees, known as the "Bronx Bombers," won the World Series again in 1941, but that year was noteworthy for other reasons. DiMaggio hit a single against the Chicago White Sox on May 15. For the next two months, he had at least one hit in every game he played—56 in a row. Through the 2011 season, that streak had never been equaled.

A few hours north of New York, the Red Sox had a left-handed hitting machine in left fielder Ted Williams. He said his goal in life was to have people one day say, "There goes Ted Williams, the greatest hitter who ever lived."

In 1941, Williams batted .406 with 37 home runs. Through the 2011 season, he is the last player to hit .400 in a season. He earned it, too. Going into the last day of the season, Williams's average was at .400. He could have sat on the bench that day to protect his .400 average—after all, if he did not bat higher than .400 that day his average would dip back into the .300s. But instead, he played both games in a doubleheader and went 6-for-8.

THAT'S A NO-NO

On June 11, 1938, Johnny Vander Meer of the Cincinnati Reds threw a no-hitter against the Boston Bees. A no-hitter is a rare feat in which a pitcher throws a complete game without giving up any hits. After just three days of rest, Vander Meer threw another no-hitter, this time against the Brooklyn Dodgers. Through 2011, they were the only back-to-back no-hitters in major league history.

Along with being the last player to hit over .400 in a season, Ted Williams is the only player since World War II to have a career batting average over .340.

QUOTABLE

"I just didn't want to be at home playing baseball while all my fellow countrymen were out fighting and serving the country." —Dom DiMaggio, who was a Boston Red Sox outfielder during the 1940s and early 1950s and the brother of Yankees star Joe DiMaggio. Dom DiMaggio served in the Navy from 1943 to 1945.

Off to War

The news was not all good that year, though. On December 7, 1941, the Japanese bombed Pearl Harbor, a US naval base in Hawaii. The United States was at war. Soon, many of the country's best ballplayers were trading baseball uniforms for military fatigues as they left to fight in World War II.

Hank Greenberg, who hit 58 home runs for the Detroit Tigers in 1938, joined the Army. Bob Feller, a 23-year-old pitching sensation for the Cleveland Indians, joined the Navy. Williams became a pilot in the Air Force. He is the only player in the Baseball Hall of Fame who served in both World War II and the Korean War.

When the troops went to war, baseball went, too. Servicemen carved out ball fields wherever they could—on a field in France or on a Pacific island. It helped them stay in shape. It kept their mind off the war. And it gave them a taste of home. Famous major leaguers played for military teams. Troops saw their baseball heroes up close. It was great for morale.

Back home, many wondered: Should Major League Baseball even go on with the nation at war? Absolutely, said the United States' number one baseball fan, President Franklin D. Roosevelt. In a letter to the commissioner of baseball in 1942, Roosevelt wrote, "I honestly feel that it would be best for the country to keep baseball going." Baseball gave people jobs, he explained. Plus, everyone was working harder because of the war, and baseball gave them a chance to relax. This became known as baseball's famous "Green Light Letter," as it gave the sport a "green light" to go on.

The games would indeed go on. But who would play? Teams needed to fill rosters, so they turned to players too old or too

ALL-AMERICAN GIRLS BASEBALL LEAGUE

Baseball is not just for boys. That was especially true during World War II. Chicago Cubs owner Philip Wrigley thought the major leagues might shut down because many players were overseas. He figured fans would still want to watch baseball, though, so he formed the All-American Girls Professional Baseball League in 1943. The league began with four teams in 1943. It grew to 10 teams based in Midwestern states such as Illinois, Wisconsin, and Indiana. After the war ended and players returned, interest in the women's league gradually faded. The league folded after the 1954 season. It was not forgotten, though. The 1992 film *A League of Their Own* was a fictional story about players in the All-American Girls Professional Baseball League.

Dorothy Kamenshek starred for the Rockford Peaches in the All-American Girls Professional Baseball League.

young for the military. In 1944, the Cincinnati Reds signed pitcher Joe Nuxhall. He was just 15 years old. Nuxhall is still the youngest player to have ever played in the major leagues.

World War II ended in 1945. Victorious US troops and ballplayers came home, and all seemed normal again. But two years later, baseball would change in a huge way.

CHAPTER 4

BLACK AND WHITE

After World War II, the United States was united in victory. Or so it seemed. The truth is, the nation was still terribly divided. In many places, especially in the South, blacks and whites lived separate lives. This included baseball. No major league organizations would hire black players.

As a result, separate leagues for black players formed. These leagues had some tremendous players. The most famous was pitcher Leroy "Satchel" Paige. The tall, lanky right-hander could deliver fastballs with pinpoint control. He was also a showman who played up to the crowds.

Still, Paige was not welcomed by white society. In 1935, Paige signed with a semi-pro team in Bismarck, North Dakota, that

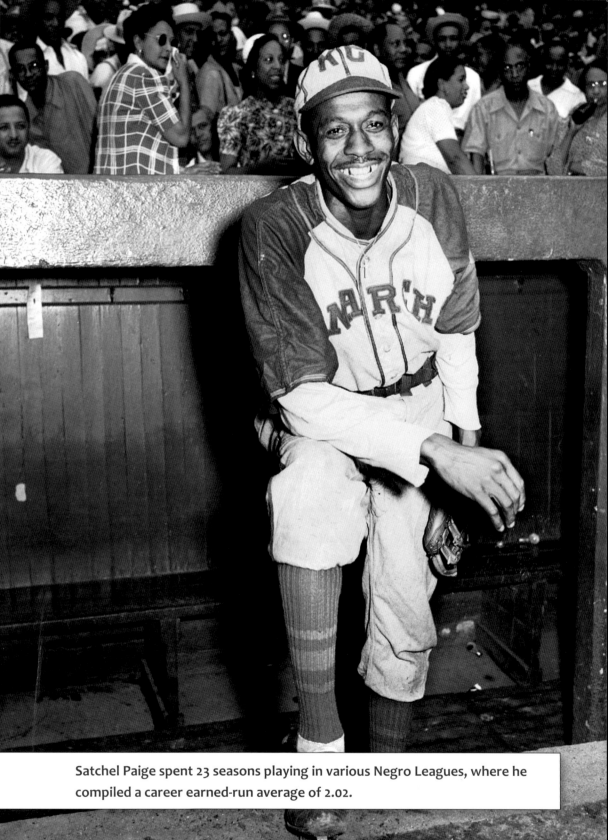

Satchel Paige spent 23 seasons playing in various Negro Leagues, where he compiled a career earned-run average of 2.02.

NEGRO LEAGUES TO THE MAJORS

After Jackie Robinson integrated baseball, some Negro League stars played in the major leagues. Pitcher Satchel Paige, by then in his 40s, played parts of six major league seasons. He went 28–31, with an earned-run average (ERA) of 3.29. That meant he gave up an average of 3.29 runs per nine innings. But other players, such as Cool Papa Bell and Buck O'Neil, never got the chance to play in the major leagues. Teams figured those players were too old. Fans can only wonder how they would have done.

had both black and white players. But when he arrived in North Dakota, no one would rent him a room. So he and his wife lived in an abandoned railway car.

Paige played most of his career in the Negro Leagues, which were the best of the leagues for black players. The Negro Leagues had other stars, too. James "Cool Papa" Bell stole 175 bases in 1933. And catcher Josh Gibson is considered one of the Negro Leagues' greatest power hitters. Statistics do not exist for all his games, but it is estimated that he hit hundreds of home runs.

Reporters covering these players began to question why they were not allowed to play in the major leagues. So did Happy Chandler, who became baseball's commissioner in 1945. He noted that many black soldiers had served in World War II. If they could fight for in the United States, Chandler said, they should be able to play baseball in the United States.

Jackie Robinson is the only player to ever have his jersey number retired by all of Major League Baseball. Robinson wore No. 42.

Jackie Robinson

Around that time, Branch Rickey, the general manager of the Brooklyn Dodgers, met Jackie Robinson. Robinson had been a star athlete at the University of California, Los Angeles. In his first Negro League season in 1945, he was an All-Star shortstop for the Kansas City Monarchs.

Rickey knew Robinson could play. But Rickey needed to know something else: Could Robinson handle the pressure of being the major leagues' first black player? Rickey explained to Robinson that Robinson's life as a major leaguer would be very hard. Fans might say terrible things to him and other players might try to hurt him when he batted or ran the bases. Rickey told him: "I want a player with guts enough *not* to fight back."

Rickey determined Robinson was that player and signed him in October 1945. When Robinson reported to spring training in Florida the following year, he could not stay at the same hotel as his teammates because it was segregated. Robinson played the 1946 season for Montreal, the Dodgers' top minor league team. He hit a home run in his first game. And for the season, he hit .349 and stole 40 bases.

On April 15, 1947, an anxious, curious baseball world watched as Robinson made his major league debut for the Dodgers. It was a very hard year for him. As Rickey had predicted, Robinson endured horrible insults, sometimes from his own teammates. But as Robinson promised, he never fought back.

THE SHOT HEARD ROUND THE WORLD

In 1951, the Brooklyn Dodgers and the New York Giants finished with identical 96–58 records. To decide the NL pennant, the teams played a best-of-three series. In the deciding Game 3, the Giants were losing 4–2 in the bottom of the ninth. With two outs, Giants batter Bobby Thomson hit a three-run home run to win the game, the series, and the pennant. Thomson's home run came to be known as the "Shot Heard Round the World." It is considered one of baseball's most famous plays. That might be because it was the first baseball game that was televised coast to coast.

PITCHER PERFECT

For a pitcher, there is no feat better than a perfect game. That means none of the batters he faced reached base. In a nine-inning perfect game, the pitcher faces 27 batters and gets all 27 batters out. Through 2010, there had been just 20 thrown in major league history. The New York Yankees' Don Larsen is the only player to throw a perfect game in the World Series, which he did in 1956.

If all the taunts and insults bothered him, he never showed it. Robinson hit .297 and helped Brooklyn win the NL pennant. Two years later, he was the NL MVP. Despite Robinson's success, teams did not rush out to sign black players. But even so, Robinson had opened the door for a new generation of baseball stars.

Going West

By 1957, the Dodgers' home ballpark, Ebbets Field, was outdated. The New York Giants, meanwhile, were having trouble drawing fans at the Polo Grounds, their aging home ballpark. Politicians in the California cities of Los Angeles and San Francisco offered the teams new stadiums and more money to head west. So, before the 1958 season, the Dodgers moved to Los Angeles and the Giants moved to San Francisco. MLB now stretched from coast to coast.

New York, which still had the Yankees, was not a one-team town for long. In 1962, the expansion Metropolitans, or Mets, came along. Since they start from scratch, most expansion teams struggle early. The Mets were especially bad. They went 40–120 in their first season. They lost more than 100 games in five of their first seven seasons. Then came 1969.

After a so-so start, the Mets began winning. They kept winning. They won the NL pennant. Then the "Amazin' Mets" stunned the favored Baltimore Orioles to win the World Series. Pitcher Tom Seaver was the star of the team. Another Mets pitcher was 22-year-old Nolan Ryan. He would later set all-time records for strikeouts (5,714) and no-hitters (7).

Hammerin' Hank

From the mid-1950s through the mid-1970s, Hank Aaron was smacking balls out of every ballpark in sight. Aaron had been playing in the Negro Leagues as an 18-year-old when the Boston Braves of the major leagues signed him in 1952. He made his big league debut in 1954, after the Braves moved to Milwaukee. Soon, he was trotting toward Babe Ruth's career home-run record.

Many people did not want Aaron to break Ruth's record. To them, Ruth was the best baseball player of all time. They wanted

Hank Aaron hits his 715th career home run in a game against the Los Angeles Dodgers.

him to remain the home-run king. And many did not want to see a black player break the record. Some fans even sent hate mail to Aaron.

But "Hammerin' Hank" Aaron marched on. On April 8, 1974, he smashed his 715th homer to pass Ruth in the record books. Aaron played two more seasons and finished his career with 755 home runs. That record stood for nearly 30 years before Barry Bonds broke it. By then, a new, controversial era of power baseball had arrived.

CHAPTER 5

HOME RUN DERBY

Hank Aaron's home-run record was doomed. The sluggers of the 1990s would make sure of that. But before that happened, another of baseball's most cherished records was shattered. Pete Rose, a dive-in-the-dirt, play-hard-every-minute bulldog, chased down Ty Cobb's all-time record of 4,189 hits. Rose, who played most of his career for the Cincinnati Reds, finished in 1986 with 4,256 hits. But his career ended in disgrace.

Rose, who had become the Reds' manager, placed bets on his team. In 1989, while he was still managing the Reds, Rose was officially banned for life from baseball. As such, baseball's all-time hits leader is not eligible for the Hall of Fame. Rose denied the allegations for years. But in 2004, he admitted that he had indeed bet on baseball games while managing the Reds.

Pete Rose runs through Ray Fosse to score the winning run in the 1970 All-Star Game. Rose's nickname, "Charlie Hustle," stemmed from his all-out approach.

Rickey Henderson stole more bases and scored more runs than any other player in baseball history.

Full Speed Ahead

Baseball has always been a game combining power and speed. During the 1980s, speed ruled. Oakland Athletics outfielder Rickey Henderson had a record 130 stolen bases in 1982. And outfielder Vince Coleman stole more than 100 bases three years in a row for the St. Louis Cardinals, from 1985 to 1987.

The 1985 Cardinals had a big, spacious ballpark and a simple strategy: Hit the ball into the gaps between outfielders and let Coleman and his teammates scorch the base paths. That formula led to the NL pennant. The plan hit a snag, though, in the World Series against the Kansas City Royals. The Cardinals were winning in Game 6 when an umpire made an incorrect call. His mistake allowed the Royals to continue batting and they eventually took the lead and the game. They then won Game 7 to take the World Series.

Perhaps no one has ever combined power and speed better than Barry Bonds. In 1990, Bonds hit 33 home runs and stole 52 bases. Over the next decade, Bonds established himself as baseball's best player. Bonds was named NL MVP seven times, including four times in a row from 2001 to 2004. No other player has achieved that since baseball began giving out MVP Awards in 1911.

Power Surge

During the 1990s, home runs flew out of ballparks like missiles. In 1998, Mark McGwire of St. Louis and Sammy Sosa of the Chicago Cubs put on a spectacular

MINOR LEAGUES

Even the best players start their professional baseball careers in the minor leagues. Players in the minors often face low pay and long bus rides to small stadiums in small towns. Each major league team has a minor league system that works like steps on a ladder. As a player gets better, he moves up the ladder toward the major leagues. The lowest rung on the ladder is the rookie leagues. Moving up, players will usually play in Class A, Class AA, and Class AAA before reaching the big leagues. There are also independent minor leagues that are not affiliated with MLB clubs.

Barry Bonds won his second MVP Award with the Pittsburgh Pirates in 1992. He would go on to win a record seven MVP Awards in his career.

power show. One massive blast after another, these two sluggers chased Roger Maris's record of 61 home runs in a season. Their home-run duel created a media frenzy. Eventually, they both passed Maris. McGwire finished with 70 home runs that year, and Sosa hit 66. They both hit more than 60 again the next year.

Then Bonds, who was noticeably bigger than he had been early in his career, topped everyone when he launched 73 home runs in 2001. That was still the single-season record following the 2011 season.

Sluggers with bulging muscles were suddenly everywhere. They earned millions of dollars and fans poured into ballparks to see them. Owners loved it, as more fans meant more money. Baseball's commissioner also loved it. After the terrible strike in 1994, baseball was again the talk of the sports world.

It seemed to be baseball at its best. But it might have been baseball at its worst. Many of the sluggers credited weight training and nutrition for their power surge. However, many of them had help from steroids and other illegal performance-enhancing drugs (PEDs).

All steroids had been declared illegal in baseball in 1991. Steroids are known to build muscle and strength. Players say they also help them recover more quickly from injuries. But they also can cause serious health problems.

Through the 1990s, players were not tested for steroid use even though the substances had been banned. But that started to

GOING BATTY

Baseball bats come in a variety of sizes, and there is no one perfect size for everyone. Youth league players can use aluminum bats, which are stronger and lighter than the wooden bats used in professional leagues. Also, an aluminum bat has a larger "sweet spot," giving the hitter a better chance to make good contact.

Mark McGwire and Sammy Sosa are linked by the 1998 home-run chase between the two sluggers and the steroid scandal that followed.

change in 2003. Investigators learned that a California company had been supplying steroids to top athletes, including some baseball players. Drug testing became more common in baseball.

In 2003, more than 100 active players tested positive—meaning they had used PEDs. The players' names were supposed to remain private, but some were published in the media.

In 2005, a former slugger and teammate of McGwire's, Jose Canseco, wrote a book claiming that steroid use in baseball was common. A lot of people did not believe him. But his claims made other people take notice. In 2007, MLB issued the Mitchell

SMALL BALL

Baseball's steroid era seemed to idolize huge, muscle-bound players. Yet many smaller players have succeeded, too. Boston Red Sox second baseman Dustin Pedroia, who was the AL MVP in 2008, is 5-feet-9 and weighs 180 pounds. Infielder David Eckstein is 5-feet-7. He played in the majors for 10 years. Eckstein was even the World Series MVP in 2006 with the St. Louis Cardinals.

Report, which linked more than 80 players to PEDs. Those players were named.

Stars Mired in Scandal

Some of the sport's biggest stars—Bonds, McGwire, Sosa, pitcher Roger Clemens, and slugging infielder Alex Rodriguez—were now linked to the use of PEDs.

Bonds has always maintained that he received lotions from a trainer; if they were steroids, he did not know it. Sosa and Clemens have said they had no chemical help. McGwire and Rodriguez both denied using PEDs, as well. Later, however, they admitted that they had.

"I was young. I was stupid. I was naïve," Rodriguez said. "And I wanted to prove to everyone that I was worth being one of the greatest players of all time."

Not all power hitters were linked to PEDs. Jim Thome hit his 600th career home run in 2011 and was never linked to steroid use.

This news left fans bitter all over again. The great home-run chase of 1998 suddenly had a different flavor. Were McGwire and Sosa cheating that season? Was Bonds cheating? Was everyone cheating? What should happen to the revered records that had been broken during this era?

Baseball has worked hard to clean up from the "steroid era." MLB has stricter tests to determine if a player is using. The penalties for using PEDs are also more severe.

DOING THE LEG WORK

Despite popular belief, pitching is not all about arm strength. "The push from your legs is probably half, or even 60 percent, of your strength on the mound," former All-Star Pedro Martinez said. "If you have strong legs and use them the right way, you will get really good velocity. And it all begins with the push off the rubber. Everything comes from the legs. That's why you have to make sure you strengthen your legs before you do any type of throwing."

A batter will often say that he needs to forget his last at-bat and focus only on the next one. In its own right, MLB has done that over and over. It has moved past gambling scandals and racism. It has moved past player strikes. Now it is working hard to move past its steroid era.

CHAPTER 6

A GLOBAL GAME

Once Jackie Robinson and other black players were allowed in the majors in the late 1940s, baseball could finally, truly be called America's pastime. By the 1960s, MLB had become a global league.

Baseball has been played around the world since the late 1800s. One of the first countries to play was Cuba, an island country in the Caribbean, just south of Florida. US sailors stopped in Cuban ports to buy and trade goods such as sugar cane. While there, the sailors played baseball and taught the game to the locals. Cubans then spread *el beisbol* to Puerto Rico, the Dominican Republic, Venezuela, and elsewhere in the region. At about the same time, half a world away, Americans showed baseball to students in Japan. Soon, Japanese teams were forming.

Babe Ruth sits with the ball boys during a 1936 exhibition game at Koshien Stadium in Osaka, Japan.

Before 1947, there were few opportunities for foreigners in American baseball. No teams would hire blacks or players with darker skin from Caribbean nations. The Cincinnati Reds, however, did sign two Cubans in 1911. They told their fans the light-skinned players were white.

Coming to America

At first, many fans did not think people from other countries could be as good as Americans in baseball. But that started to change in 1951. Chico Carrasquel from Venezuela and Minnie Minoso from Cuba both were named All-Stars that year. Soon, more and more players from Latin America were coming to the United States to play.

In 1955, a 20-year-old from Puerto Rico named Roberto Clemente joined the Pittsburgh Pirates. Clemente led the league

"CITY OF SHORTSTOPS"

San Pedro de Marcoris, a city in the Dominican Republic, is known for two things: sugar cane and baseball players. With about 220,000 people living there, the city is much smaller than big cities in the United States. Yet it has produced more than 80 major league players. In the 1980s, it became known as the "city of shortstops" because several major league middle infielders at that time all came from the town. Other more recent players from San Pedro include Sammy Sosa, Alfonso Soriano, and Robinson Cano.

Roberto Clemente was the NL batting champ four times and was named the NL MVP in 1966.

in batting four times and was named an All-Star 12 times. He helped Pittsburgh win two World Series titles. His Hall of Fame career ended tragically, though. In 1972, he was traveling to Nicaragua with some relief supplies after an earthquake. The plane he was in crashed and Clemente was killed.

Since the days of Clemente, Latin American players often have played a big part in a team's success. The 1970s Cincinnati Reds are a great example. The "Big Red Machine," as the team was known, romped to World Series wins in 1975 and 1976.

In 2001, Seattle Mariners outfielder Ichiro Suzuki became just the second player to win Rookie of the Year and MVP honors in the same season.

The Reds had three Latin Americans from three different countries in their starting lineup—first baseman Tony Perez (Cuba), shortstop Dave Concepcion (Venezuela), and center fielder Cesar Geronimo (Dominican Republic).

Made in Japan

Baseball in Japan has flourished since the early 1900s. Its professional league is excellent. Most experts consider it to be the best outside of the major leagues in the United States. But it was not until 1964 that Masanori Murakami, a relief pitcher for the San Francisco Giants, became the first Japanese native to play in the major leagues. Hideo Nomo, another pitcher, came to the United States in 1995 and was an MLB All-Star in his first season.

No Japanese player has had a greater impact than Ichiro Suzuki, though. He had been one of the best hitters ever in Japan. His move to the Seattle Mariners in 2001 was huge news. Fans wondered: Could he hit top MLB pitching as well as he hit Japanese pitching? They did not have to wait long for an answer.

In his first season with Seattle, Ichiro hit .350 and led the AL in hits and batting average. He was named the AL Rookie of the Year and MVP. In 2004, he set a major league record with 262 hits. Back home, Ichiro remains a hero in a country that loves baseball.

GLOBAL COMPETITION

Baseball has appeared on and off at the Olympic Games since 1904. It often was a demonstration sport, meaning no medals were awarded. It became a medal sport for the 1992 Games and stayed that way for several years. Cuba won the gold medal in 1992, 1996, and 2004. The United States won in 2000. And South Korea captured gold in 2008. However, the International Olympic Committee voted to remove baseball from the Olympics after that year. Because the Summer Games take place during the MLB season, the best players in the world did not participate. As such, the Olympic baseball competition sometimes struggled to draw fan interest.

All was not lost, though. In 2006, the World Baseball Classic debuted as a new tournament for national baseball teams. Because it took place in the United States and during MLB's spring training, many of the top MLB players competed. Japan won the first two tournaments, in 2006 and 2009.

Bonkers about *Beisbol*

Perhaps no nation is crazier about baseball than the Dominican Republic. Many Dominican boys are poor, but they play the game anywhere they can—in open fields, in parks, or even on dusty streets. Many children do not have gloves or a ball or a bat. Instead, they pitch a bottle cap or a balled-up sock and try to hit it with a broom handle. They imagine they are the next Pedro Martinez, Vladimir Guerrero, or Alfonso Soriano. All three of them were MLB stars during the late-1990s and early-2000s. And all three are Dominican.

The baseball-crazed Dominican is smaller than West Virginia, but it has produced more than 500 major leaguers, including about 90 in 2010. It is nearly impossible to go to a major league or minor league game today and not see at least one Dominican player.

THE WINTER LEAGUES

When cold and snow blankets much of the United States, the winter league season in the Caribbean heats up. The Dominican Republic, Mexico, Venezuela, and Puerto Rico all have popular winter baseball leagues. Some Latin American major leaguers return to play in the winter in their home countries. Minor leaguers also play in the winter leagues. They hope to improve their skills so they can reach the majors. Each February, the champions of the four winter leagues meet in the *Series del Caribe*, which means "The Caribbean Series" in Spanish.

The Cardinals' Albert Pujols hits a home run in Game 1 of the 2006 World Series. A three-time NL MVP, Pujols hails from the Dominican Republic.

Major league teams are always on the lookout for the next Dominican star. Most MLB teams have academies in the country. These are baseball schools for talented Dominican teenagers. The goal of all these boys is the same: To one day make it to *las grandes ligas*, which means "the major leagues" in Spanish.

Very few who play baseball ever make the major leagues. Yet millions of people of all ages play the game every year. Millions more watch at ballparks and on television. From dusty lots in the Dominican Republic to gleaming stadiums in big US cities, the game goes on, just as it has since the New York Knickerbockers knocked around a beat-up ball in the 1800s.

TIMELINE

1778 Revolutionary War soldiers at Valley Forge play a game called "base."

1845 The New York Knickerbockers produce the first set of baseball rules. Many differ from today's rules, but some are very similar.

1869 The Cincinnati Red Stockings become the first professional baseball team.

1903 The first World Series is played. In a best-of-nine format, the Boston Americans defeat the Pittsburgh Pirates, five games to three.

1911 The Cincinnati Reds sign the first two Cuban baseball players.

1919 The Reds upset the Chicago White Sox to win the World Series. It is later learned that several key White Sox were paid by gamblers to lose the series on purpose. It becomes known as the Black Sox Scandal.

1920 Boston Red Sox owner Harry Frazee sells Babe Ruth to the New York Yankees for $125,000.

1927 Behind Ruth's record-setting 60 home runs and a batting order known as "Murderers Row," the Yankees finish the season 110–44 and win the World Series.

1935 The Reds beat the Philadelphia Phillies 2–1 in the major leagues' first night game.

1941 Joe DiMaggio hits safely in 56 straight games. Ted Williams goes six-for-eight in a doubleheader on the last day of the season to finish with a batting average of .406.

1942 President Franklin D. Roosevelt issues his "Green Light Letter," encouraging baseball to continue during World War II.

1947 Jackie Robinson plays first base for the Brooklyn Dodgers on April 15. He becomes the first black player in the major leagues.

1957 Baseball expands to the West. The New York Giants announce they are moving to San Francisco, and the Brooklyn Dodgers announce they are moving to Los Angeles before the 1958 season.

1961 Roger Maris hits his 61st home run, breaking Ruth's single-season record.

1974 Hank Aaron hits his 715th career home run on April 8 to break Ruth's career record.

1982 Cal Ripken Jr. joins the Baltimore Orioles' starting lineup on May 30. He won't leave it for another 15 years.

1985 Pete Rose breaks Ty Cobb's record for career hits.

1994 Players go on strike on August 12. The strike lasts through the end of the season. For the first time since 1904, there is no World Series.

1998 Mark McGwire and Sammy Sosa both break Maris's single-season home-run record of 61. McGwire finishes with 70; Sosa hits 66. On September 20, Ripken sits out a game, ending a streak of 2,632 consecutive games played.

2003 More than 100 players test positive for PEDs. Their names are not released, but the total leads to further testing.

2004 The Boston Red Sox sweep the St. Louis Cardinals to win the World Series. It is the franchise's first World Series win since Ruth was sold to the Yankees 84 years earlier.

2010 The San Francisco Giants defeat the Texas Rangers in the World Series. It is the Giants' first title since moving from New York in 1958.

LEGENDS OF BASEBALL

Hank Aaron
outfielder

Johnny Bench
catcher

Yogi Berra
catcher

Barry Bonds
outfielder

Roberto Clemente
outfielder

Ty Cobb
outfielder

Joe DiMaggio
outfielder

Jimmie Foxx
first baseman

Lou Gehrig
first baseman

Lefty Grove
pitcher

Rogers Hornsby
second baseman

Walter Johnson
pitcher

Sandy Koufax
pitcher

Mickey Mantle
outfielder

Christy Mathewson
pitcher

Willie Mays
outfielder

John McGraw
third baseman, shortstop,
manager

Stan Musial
outfielder,
first baseman

Satchel Paige
pitcher

Kirby Puckett
outfielder

Cal Ripken Jr.
shortstop,
third baseman

Frank Robinson
outfielder

Jackie Robinson
second baseman,
first baseman

Pete Rose
outfielder, first base,
third base

Babe Ruth
outfielder, pitcher

Nolan Ryan
pitcher

Warren Spahn
pitcher

Ichiro Suzuki
outfielder

Honus Wagner
shortstop

Ted Williams
outfielder

Cy Young
pitcher

GLOSSARY

ace
A team's top starting pitcher.

attendance
The number of fans who attend a game, a series, or a season.

base paths
The areas between bases used by runners to advance around the field.

debut
A first appearance.

doubleheader
A set of two baseball games played between the same two teams on the same day.

durability
The ability to stay healthy.

expansion
When a team or teams are added to a league.

pennant
A long, triangular flag. In baseball, the word is used to describe a league championship.

perfect game
A game in which a pitcher retires every batter from the opposing team. In a nine-inning game, that means the pitcher faces 27 batters and gets them all out.

professional
Someone who is paid to work.

salary cap
A pay structure for professional players in which the total amount of money paid to players would be limited.

tee
A stand on which players set a baseball before hitting the ball. They are used by beginners who are learning the game as well as experienced players for batting practice.

velocity
Rate of motion; speed.

warning track
A section of dirt or synthetic rubber that runs the length of the field between the outfield grass and the fence.

FOR MORE INFORMATION

Selected Bibliography

Anton, Todd and Bill Nowlin, editors. *When Baseball Went To War*. Chicago: Triumph Books, 2008. Print.

Asinof, Eliot. *Eight Men Out*. New York: Henry Holt and Co., 1963. Print.

Gillette, Gary and Pete Palmer, eds. *The ESPN Baseball Encyclopedia*. 5th ed. New York: Sterling Publishing, 2008. Print.

Lorimer, Lawrence. *Baseball Desk Reference*. New York: DK Publishing, 2002. Print.

Schlossberg, Dan. *The Baseball Almanac*. Chicago: Triumph Books, 2002. Print.

Further Readings

Krasner, Steven. *Play Ball Like The Pros*. Atlanta: Peachtree Publishers, 2002. Print.

Ripken, Cal Jr., Bill Ripken with Larry Burke. *Play Baseball The Ripken Way*. New York: Random House, 2004. Print.

Vecsey, George. *Baseball: A History of America's Favorite Game*. New York: Modern Library, 2008. Print.

Web Links

To learn more about baseball, visit ABDO Publishing Company online at **www.abdopublishing.com**. Web sites about baseball are featured on our Book Links page. These links are routinely monitored and updated to provide the most current information available.

Places to Visit

National Baseball Hall of Fame and Museum

25 Main Street
Cooperstown, NY 13326
(888) HALL-OF-FAME
www.baseballhall.org
This hall of fame and museum highlights the greatest players and moments in the history of baseball. Among the legends enshrined there are Ty Cobb, Willie Mays, Jackie Robinson, Babe Ruth, and Cy Young.

Negro Leagues Baseball Museum

1616 East 18th Street
Kansas City, MO 64108
(816) 221-1920
www.nlbm.com
This museum features photographs, artifacts, and other multimedia displays that honor the rich history of the Negro Leagues.

INDEX

About the Author

Bo Smolka is a former sports copy editor at the *Baltimore Sun*. He is also a former college sports information director and magazine editor. Smolka has received several national writing awards from the College Sports Information Directors of America (CoSIDA), including CoSIDA's National Story of the Year in 1996. His work has appeared in USAToday.com, *National Geographic World*, and many other national publications. Smolka lives in Baltimore, Maryland, with his wife and two children. When he's not writing, he can often be found coaching his son's baseball teams.